Cracker Jack Prizes

Cracker Jack Prizes

by Alex Jaramillo

Conceived and designed by
Cooper Edens, Welleran Poltarnees, and Alexandra Day

Photography by
John Snedeker and C. L. Haines

Abbeville Press · Publishers · New York

Editor: Walton Rawls
Design Associate: Stephanie Bart-Horvath
Production Supervisor: Hope Koturo

Library of Congress Cataloging-in-Publication Data

Jaramillo, Alex.
  Crackerjack prizes.

  1. Cracker Jack (Firm)—History.
2. Popcorn industry—United States—History.
3. Collectibles—United States. I. Title.
II. Title: Cracker Jack prizes.
HD9049.P652U65   1989   338.7′664805677   88-34282
ISBN 1-55859-000-5

We thank the noted Cracker Jack collector Wes Johnson of
Louisville, Kentucky, for allowing us to photograph the ads
on page 26, and on the back cover for use in this book.

Table of Contents

The History, Appeal, and Prizes of Cracker Jack   6

The 1910s: Experimentation   16

The 1920s: The Golden Age Begins   22

The 1930s: The Golden Age Continues   34

The 1940s: The War Years   46

The 1950s: Plastic Profusion   54

The 1960s: Weathering the Storm   66

The 1970s: Within Strict Limits   76

The 1980s: Instant Gratification and Disposability   86

The History, Appeal, and Prizes of Cracker Jack

The Cracker Jack story begins with a German immigrant, Frederick William Rueckheim, who used the $200 he saved working on an Illinois farm to go into business in Chicago. In 1871, just after the Great Fire, Rueckheim opened a street stand with a partner, popping and selling popcorn. Two years later he bought out his partner and sent for his brother from Germany. The two brothers added candy and marshmallows to their thriving business and between 1875 and 1887 moved their factory six times—to meet the increasing needs of their growing business. In 1893 the World's Columbian Exposition was held in Chicago, and, like all great world's fairs, it changed the way people saw the world. Businesses and governments, as well as artists, all strained to impress, and the 21,000,000 people who flowed through the fair came out with an increased sense of the Earth's inhabitants' striving together toward transformation. At this fair most Americans saw, for the first time, a Ferris wheel, the "canals of Venice," a Mosque, a miniature Eiffel Tower, Egyptian belly

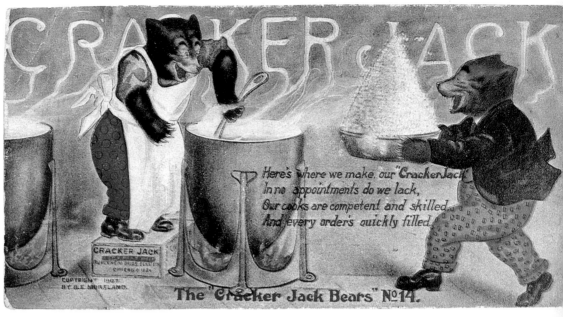

The "Cracker Jack Bears" No. 14.

dancers, and a "Lapland village" complete with reindeer. It was there also that most Americans tasted, for the first time, the Rueckheim Brothers' caramelized popcorn. After this event, their business increased so rapidly that F. W. Rueckheim observed that "No matter how we try to plan for it, the orders always exceed production."

In 1896 the brothers found a name for their enormously popular confection when a salesman, enjoying a mouthful, used the current slang phrase, "That's a Cracker Jack." The name stuck.

From the street stand in 1871 until 1899 Cracker Jack was sold exclusively in bulk. Sometimes, at a public event, it was prepared in a booth like the one shown on page 12, but more often it was produced in the factory and shipped to the retailers in large wooden tubs. In 1899 packaging

expert Henry Eckstein joined the company and developed the wax sealer and a moisture-proof package. Now Cracker Jack could be sold in handy boxes that would keep it fresh for extended periods. This made it possible for Cracker Jack to be widely distributed and to become a national favorite. The original Cracker Jack box is pictured on page 13, and Sailor Jack and Bingo were added to it in 1918. This distinctive package, and the formalization of a free prize included, gave added power to an already successful product. By 1923 all the rest of the company's candy production, except Angus Marshmallows, was dropped. In 1927, a new record was set when 137,754,000 boxes of Cracker Jack were sold.

Cracker Jack had quickly become the world's largest user of popcorn, which it popped in giant

THE HOME OF CRACKER JACK

corn-poppers two stories tall. A special hybrid popcorn that perfectly fits the company's needs is grown solely for Cracker Jack by widely scattered farmers. The peanuts are also a unique strain.

In 1948 approximately 240,000,000 boxes of Cracker Jack were sold. The company has never advertised extensively but has relied principally on memory to sell the product; sales have contin-

ued to grow with the population of the United States. Despite the fact that many of us think of Cracker Jack as an old-fashioned treat, more is sold today than ever in its history. It is clearly America's most consistently popular confection.

In 1964 the Borden company purchased Cracker Jack, and it has kept the faith. In 1975 the new owners developed a way to prepare the confection in a high-speed continuous-cooking machine, rather than in the metal tubs in which it had been cooked in individual batches since the beginning. The formula for Cracker Jack has not changed since the early 1890s, except that since the 1960s Borden has used corn syrup in place of white sugar. Today Cracker Jack is essentially the same felicitous combination of elements; and, as befits such excellence, it continues to thrive.

The "Cracker Jack Bears" Nº6.

The "Cracker Jack's" to
New York went
Their hearts were full
of good intent,
While there they found
each candy stand
Sold *Cracker Jack*
on every hand.

THE APPEAL OF CRACKER JACK

First, the name. Cracker Jack is so redolent and shapely a phrase that it is hard to imagine that it has not always been with us. *A Dictionary of Americanisms* lists its first appearance in print (in alternate form) as 1896, the same year it was applied to the product. In April of that year *The New York Herald* remarked of a baseball team that there were "so many crackajacks in the lot that . . . some good men will have to sit on the bench and wait for a chance." Thus it was very likely a fresh slang phrase when F. W. Rueckheim decided to apply it to his principal product. To judge how audacious, and unlikely, a gamble he undertook, you need only review in your own mind the short lives of recent slang expressions of exaggerated praise. By luck or wisdom he hit on a phrase that is timeless, unforgettable, and adulatory.

The box has always been a thin rectangle, but the proportions have varied from decade to decade. It is a box one can easily grow attached to. One wants to pick it up, perhaps slip it into a pocket.

In 1918, while America was engaged in the

This is the home of "Cracker Jack"
Where business never does grow slack,
We work away from morn till night,
To make our sweets and make them
right.

The "Cracker Jack Bears" Nº 13.

"Hurrah for liberty!" they cry,
Who holds the lamp of freedom high,
The only thing that she can lack
Is just a box of "Cracker Jack".

The "Cracker Jack Bears" Nº 4.

Then next they flew away to Mars,
That lies high up among the stars,
And there they found a great demand
For "Cracker Jack" on every hand.

The "Cracker Jack Bears" Nº 16.

"Delighted" said our
nation's head,
For many years your
sweets have led
All the confections of our
land,
Congratulations-here's my
hand.

The "Cracker Jack Bears" Nº7.

10

First World War, a new red-white-and-blue box was designed for Cracker Jack. Very likely the image of Cracker Jack as fundamentally American has been advanced through our largely unconscious reaction to this color scheme, which has been retained. Also on the box, for the first time, were Sailor Jack and his dog, Bingo, who were modeled after F. W. Rueckheim's grandson Robert and his dog. They had been pictured in magazine advertisements since 1916. Shortly after the package was introduced Robert died of pneumonia. On his gravestone there is a picture of him in his sailor suit.

The complex appeal of any image is difficult to analyze. This picture of a sailor boy standing feet apart and saluting us, his dog's chain tangled around his leg, is a powerful one. But boys are not really sailors; they wear sailor suits because of

adoring parents. This one has "Cracker Jack" emblazoned on his cap, which invites us to think of Cracker Jack as a ship, even a navy, in which children are the crew. This particular "jack," a common term for a sailor, holds an uncomfortably large armload of Cracker Jack boxes, one of the more obvious promotion devices. His dog is

11

named Bingo, probably because that's what you cry out when you win the prize. Bingo's tangled leash suggests a real happening, not a commercial pose. Jack's wide stance is, to me, an indication of his openness and sincerity. Finally, there is his salute. He recognizes us. We are not merely one of a faceless multitude. We are seen and acknowledged by a sweet child who is engaged in the mission of spreading Cracker Jack and cheer to a hungry world. This is what Jack and Bingo mean to me. They will mean something a little different

to each viewer, but inasmuch as we share the same culture, the impact will be similar. In addition to all of this, there is familiarity. I cannot remember what I felt when I first saw a Cracker Jack box, but now when I see one my whole lifetime,

and that of my father, get involved. In an ever-shifting reality, Cracker Jack is one of the few elements that remain. Yes, he has changed a little, but still he salutes me, and still I reach for the Cracker Jack.

The motto, "The more you eat, the more you want," is a powerful inducement. After the first encounter it bypasses our consciousness, but its simple assertion and rhythmic structure probably resound through the corridors of our being, encouraging us to buy and eat.

Popcorn is another factor in Cracker Jack's appeal. Popcorn is one of those foods associated with comfort and enjoyment. We eat it in the movies and at sports events, and it is exciting to pop at home. It is also one of those things hard to stop eating.

12

Peanuts are another element in Cracker Jack's appeal. In and of themselves they are a favorite food, something that many people cannot resist. Cracker Jack peanuts, however, are not just peanuts; they are candy-coated peanuts. Moreover, these peanuts must be searched for, and every one found is an individual triumph.

Finally, there is the molasses. Though many of us will not admit it, sugar makes everything more desirable. Two already attractive elements, beautifully sweetened, are predictably popular. Fur-

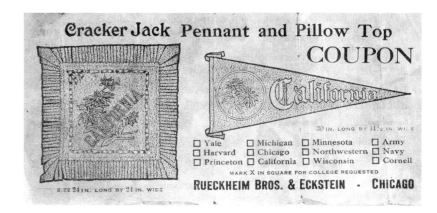

thermore, Cracker Jack doesn't just cover the product with molasses. The company has a special process that does away with stickiness, making consumption easier and more aesthetically pleasing.

All of these factors, working together, make a powerfully appealing confection. Then, on top of all this, there are the prizes.

THE PRIZES

Historians often discover that as they approach the center of an issue or the heart of a period, the information becomes scarcer, the focus less sharp. So it is with Cracker Jack. The prizes are the most important aspect of the whole—the things we remember and value—yet when we probe the origins of the idea we find obscurity. The Cracker Jack company states that in 1910 and 1911 the boxes carried a prize in every box. The truth appears not so simple. Probably all of the prizes pictured in this chapter are earlier than 1910. Very likely from the mid 1890s on the

13

Cracker Jack people experimented with inserting prizes from time to time. The badges showing beautiful ladies are certainly from the turn of the century. The metal toys were also early—and made to be discovered in a box! Prizes that were used in this period were often not produced especially for Cracker Jack and do not bear the company's name, but a great variety of evidence indicates that they were so used. The riddle card (page 14) and the Cracker Jack bear post cards (pages 8, 10, and 11) were to be found in the boxes. Both prizes offered the opportunity to complete the sets by mail, but the beginning point was the card in the box. The bear cards were copyrighted in 1907.

Coupons (like the ones on pages 12 and 13) were either printed on or included in the boxes. In the Cracker Jack archives is a 116-page catalog,

published in 1912, that lists the things you could redeem your coupons for. These included clothes, toys, and sporting goods, and all were, in a sense, Cracker Jack prizes.

Cracker Jack was not, perhaps, the first popcorn confection that included prizes. Checkers, a very similar popcorn product later absorbed by Cracker Jack, was referred to in a 1906 magazine advertisement as "the original prize popcorn." Cracker Jack may not have been the first to realize the power of "a prize in every box," but the company recognized this truth as it evolved in a variety of other ways toward a correct form and impact for its product.

One of the ways that Cracker Jack raised sales, and bested the competition, was through the device of issuing prizes in a series. Not every prize is

14

part of a series, but many, in every decade, are. What the company counted on was that a Cracker Jack customer would particularly desire to collect one line of prizes, and that this fancy would lead to the buying, opening, and searching through of a great many boxes of Cracker Jack.

The core of this volume is the presentation of the toys of Cracker Jack. The several hundred shown here were selected from the more than 5,000 in my collection. The criteria were several. First, we tried to be as certain as possible that what is shown was actually associated with Cracker Jack. For the early years it is often difficult to determine what was a Cracker Jack prize, for many candidates are unmarked and were identical to ones made for other purposes. As a collector, I always prefer prizes marked with the words Cracker Jack, and in compiling this book I exercised that same preference. The second criterion of choice was physical beauty of a kind susceptible to photographic reproduction. Many fine prizes had to be eliminated because of this. A third aspect of choice was historical significance. Some pieces represent milestones in the development of Cracker Jack prizes, others illuminate the years in which they were produced.

The chapters on the prizes are arranged chronologically by decade, for I believe that Cracker Jack prizes tell the story of our century. Probably the history of any artifact does this, for surely the greater truth is embodied in its ongoing manifestations, but Cracker Jack prizes are the ones I know best, and I display them here for your edification and delight.

BECKER, Philadelphia - National

The 1910s: Experimentation

This decade was, for the United States, a time of increasing complexity. The automobile was now owned by millions of people, and the mobility it promoted promised to change everything. More and more people left the land to live in cities, and electricity began to do much of our work for us. The moving picture show had, for the first time, a major impact on our consciousness. We became aware of how big and complicated, both for good and ill, the world had become. The seemingly simple existence of our ancestors was a thing of the past. Privation and discontent increased, and in 1914 a great war broke out in Europe. It became increasingly clear that a reluctant America would also become embroiled, and we entered the war in 1917.

The frantic diversity of life, in this decade, is reflected in Cracker Jack's prizes. Rueckheim Bros. and Eckstein came to a clear realization of the importance of prizes to the success of their product. The company decided to experiment, and the results are marvelous and manifold.

Here, more than at any other time, there were offered a significant number of prizes that would appeal to adults. The baseball cards and score counter, the book of riddles, and the book of songs; these would appeal equally to the adult and child buyer. The baby's barrette would appeal almost exclusively to the adult customer. The offerings were not only various, they were often elaborate. The paper toys (the boy eating Cracker Jack and the sliding movies) are of an astonishing ambition and fragility. The two little books are real books, not eight-page pamphlets. The whistles are well made, and still blow. The tops are of metal and spin beautifully.

INNINGS

CRACKER JACK

HOME TEAM

SCORE COUNTER

VISITING TEAM

This counter can be used in most any card game

J. S. CARROLL, CHICAGO

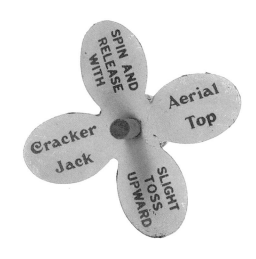

This baseball score counter and the baseball cards on page 20 testify to Cracker Jack's early connection with baseball. Obviously Cracker Jack was a familiar part of the baseball park scene well before "Take Me Out to the Ball Game" was published in 1907. With music by Albert Von Tilzer and words by Jack Norworth, the song includes the immortal line, "Buy me some peanuts and Cracker Jack." In the 1950s Jack Norworth was the official spokesman for Cracker Jack. He toured the United States and often appeared in parades in a red-white-and-blue car.

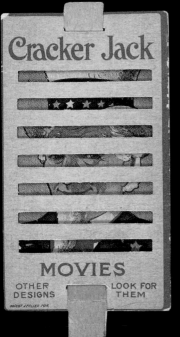

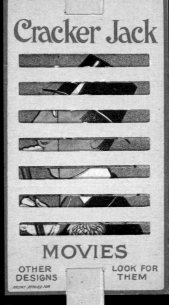

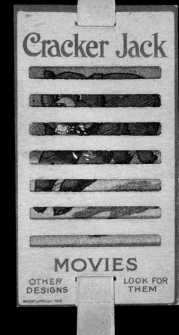

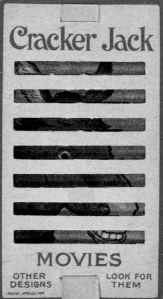

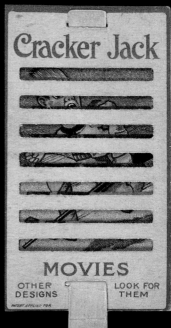

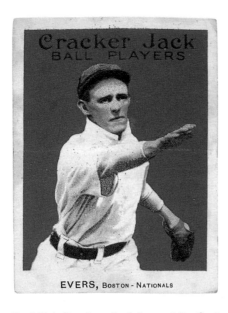

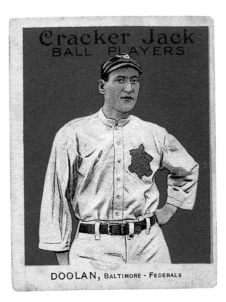

EVERS, Boston - Nationals

DOOLAN, Baltimore - Federals

CAMNITZ, Pittsburgh - Federals

In 1914 Cracker Jack issued its first set of 144 baseball cards. Obtainable only in the boxes, the cards were so popular that the next year the set was expanded to 176 cards. In 1915 one could obtain, by mail, a complete set for either 100 coupons or one coupon and ten cents. More than 15,000,000 cards were distributed. Today the cards are quite scarce and valuable. A complete set, in mint condition, would sell for around $12,000. The Ty Cobb card alone is worth about $2,000. The Cracker Jack cards included players from the short-lived Federal League.

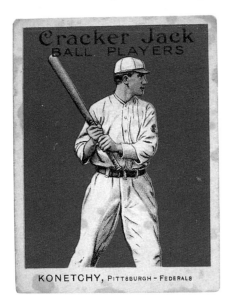

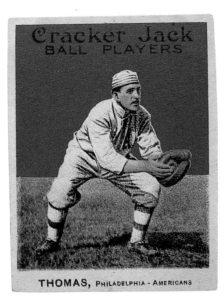

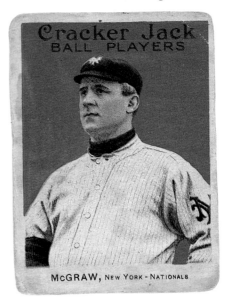

KONETCHY, Pittsburgh - Federals

THOMAS, Philadelphia - Americans

McGRAW, New York - Nationals

The 1920s:
The Golden Age Begins

Cracker Jack   "The More You
                 The Mo-e You

The First World War changed everything. Before that tragic series of events, America's basic values were Victorian; afterwards, the past seemed very far behind us. The self-denial of the war years was followed by a wave of self-indulgence. Conventional constraints on individual behavior were crumbling. There was a new spirit of "anything goes." Increased mobility and nation-wide communications reinforced the new mood. The Constitutional Amendment prohibiting the manufacture and consumption of alcohol, which was ratified in 1919, seemed to intensify the nation's pursuit of pleasure. The almost universal flaunting of the law led to an even deeper sense of individual isolation, with momentary pleasure the supreme goal.

The effect of all these social forces on Cracker Jack prizes was beneficial. What this led to was audacity and variety. The Cracker Jack company seems to have had few practical constraints on the creation of new toys. As long as it fit in the box, it was a possibility. The paper Indian headdress folds out to almost two feet in length. Many of the prizes, if purchased individually, would have cost as much or more than the five cent box of Cracker Jack. There was a real sense of adventure in every box, and what one found was always surprising, often pleasing.

The Cracker Jack Co.

CHICAGO--NEW YORK

The 1920s and '30s were the greatest years for paper doll collecting in America. Millions of little girls collected the dolls, but beyond accumulating them they also avidly played with them, creating vast wardrobes and imaginative environments. Cracker Jack issued several sets of paper dolls, and they were very popular. Oddly, the company seems not to have included Sailor Jack and Bingo, which would have been most apropos.

The Cracker Jack pocket watch was widely distributed, and still occurs with fair frequency at antique sales. With it being less ephemeral than many other prizes, one can imagine generations of children pulling the watch solemnly from a pocket when the subject of time arose.

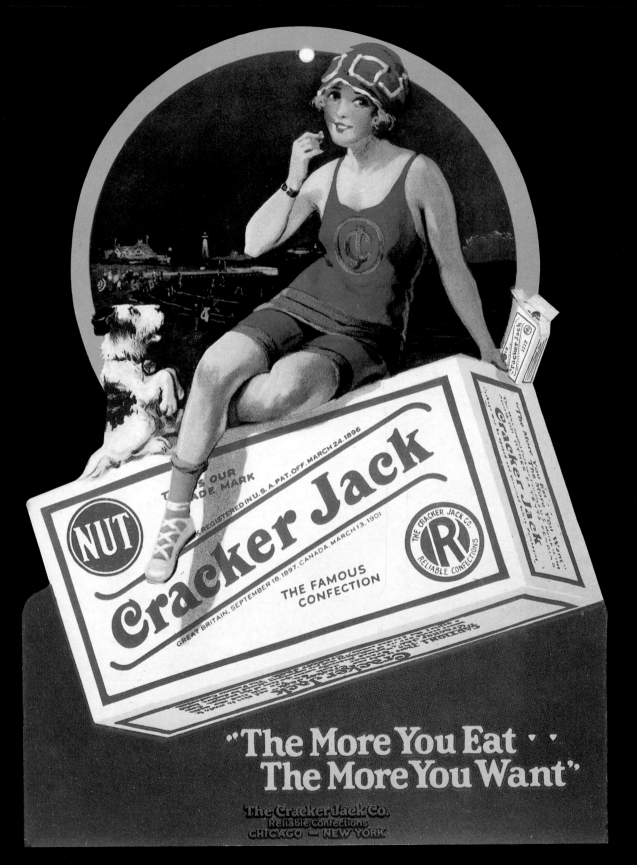

The pinball games to the left and right are both covered in celluloid, the world's first commercially successful man-made material. Patented in 1870, it was the marvel of the age.

28

29

These banks are curious in that they have so small a capacity for coins. They would certainly hold no more than five pennies, but perhaps the intention was for a child to save his coins just toward the purchase of a box of Cracker Jack.

Embossed tin toys were indeed offered in the golden years of Cracker Jack prize distribution, but they never were so abundant as people imagine. Many visualize these items when they think of a fine old Cracker Jack prize, but they always were outnumbered by paper prizes.

The *Animated Jungleland Book* was obtained by first finding the card (seen to its right) in a box of Cracker Jack and then sending ten cents to the company by mail. The book itself is a sophisticated mechanical device in which the duck flaps his wings, the donkey kicks, etc.

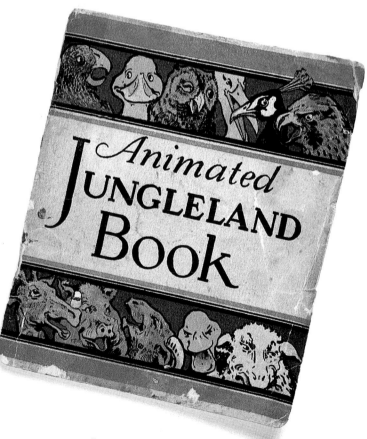

This Indian war bonnet is one of the loveliest and most fragile objects ever included in a box of Cracker Jack. When fully unfolded the bonnet is about two feet in length.

READ THIS, BOYS AND GIRLS! LOTS OF FUN FOR YOU

Cut me out of a
Cracker Jack
Package and Save

If you like this prize Wiggle Wag then you'll want the JUNGLELAND Story Book. You just wag the pages back and forth and see the animals do their stunts. Every boy and girl can easily get one.

HOW TO GET THE FUNNY BOOK
Send 10c in stamps with 5 heads of the Cracker Jack Boy to
The Cracker Jack Co.
530 S. Peoria St., Chicago, Ill.

OH, HOW YOU'LL LAUGH
Piggie Wig sings. Donkey Donk kicks. The birds do stunts. My, but you'll have a great time reading and playing with the ANIMATED JUNGLELAND Story Book.
There is nothing like it, boys and girls, and to get one, send only 10c in stamps with 5 heads of the Cracker Jack Boy cut from 5 Cracker Jack packages to
The Cracker Jack Co.
530 S. Peoria St., Chicago, Ill.

I am Red-Bird,
wag my tail,

If you would have
some fun,

Move the pages
back and forth,

That is how
it's done.

Pat. Pending

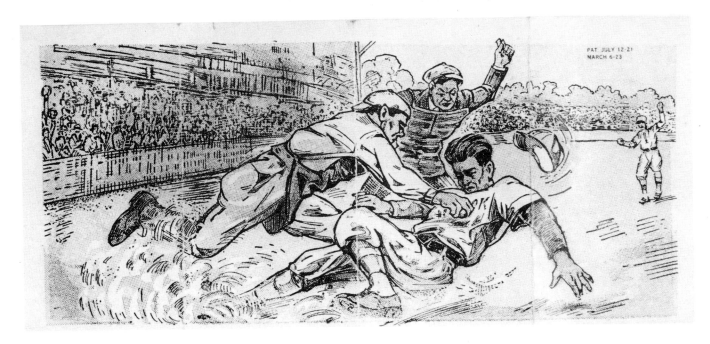

32

BASEBALL

BASEBALL is the preeminent American sport. It is the most complicated of any of the hundreds of games that have been played with a ball from the time of the anc.ent Greeks. It demands more in the way of quick action combined with quick thinking than nearly any other game. It is quicker and livelier than cricket, the English national game. A game of baseball is over in a few hours.

Baseball is said to be derived from the old English game of "rounders," by way of the New England game of "two old cat." The first regular club was founded in New York in 1845, but it was not until after the civil war that it spread over the whole country, until in the seventies that nearly every town in the country has its team. There be organized, until today when nearly every town in the country has its team. There Amateur baseball is played mostly by the colleges, all of which have teams. There are few things in America that create such general excitement and interest as the World's Series.

Directions—To paint the picture use brush and clean water, rinsing the brush after painting each part. Keep carefully within the black outlines. Paint without paint.

Made in U.S.A.

Cracker Jack

"THE MORE YOU EAT- THE MORE YOU WANT"

REG. U.S. PAT. OFF.

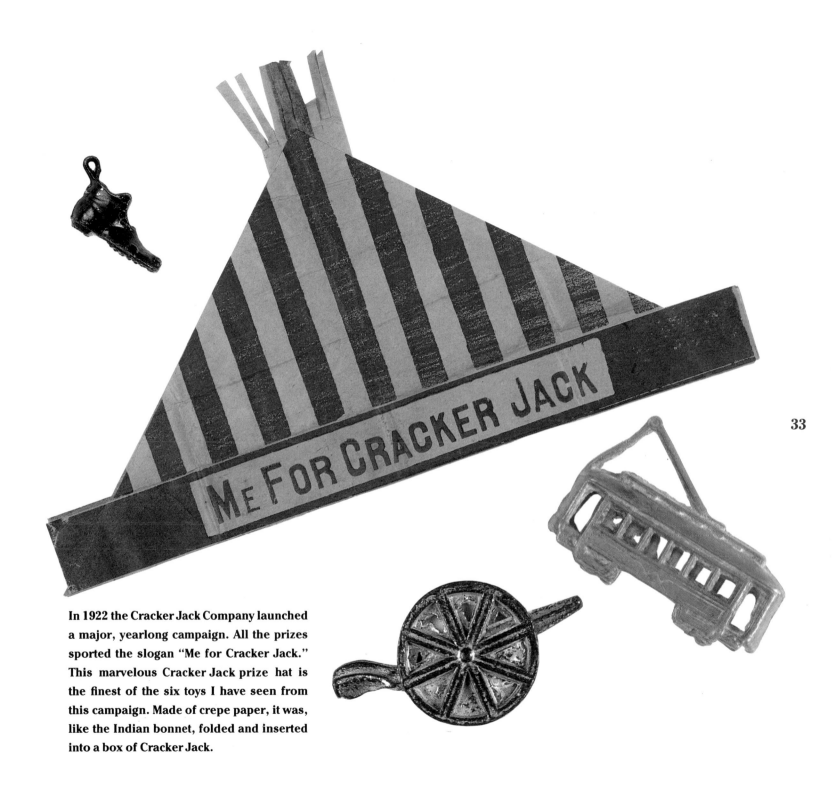

In 1922 the Cracker Jack Company launched a major, yearlong campaign. All the prizes sported the slogan "Me for Cracker Jack." This marvelous Cracker Jack prize hat is the finest of the six toys I have seen from this campaign. Made of crepe paper, it was, like the Indian bonnet, folded and inserted into a box of Cracker Jack.

The 1930s: The Golden Age Continues

This decade is an anomaly. Throughout it America was gripped by a severe economic depression. There was vast unemployment, and for most of the decade individual incomes were less than half what they had been in the 1920s. In the decade's second half we were haunted by the rise and violence of Fascism in Europe and the growing likelihood that another world war would engulf us. One would expect, under these circumstances, that cultural manifestations would have been shadowed and stingy, but, instead, there was a great outpouring of vitality in the popular arts. Hollywood's movies were often splendid, sometimes magnificent. Our greatest stars and film studios developed and flowered. Songwriting flourished; Gershwin, Berlin, and Porter were all in full stride. The stage was lively and innovative. Radio, which was now national, became ingenious and diversified, and it played a significant role in the daily life of most American families. Magazines and newspapers were sold in great numbers. Individual spirit clearly refused to be defeated by political and economic disasters.

Cracker Jack shared this cultural efflorescence. The company experimented with new products; Cracker Jack brittle, Popcorn Crisp, Zulu Bars, Mallow Whip and Cream, chocolate-covered Cracker Jack, Nut Bits, Lik-Rish Jack, and French-Fried Popcorn were all tried. In 1932, "The Cracker Jack Mystery Club" was founded, and it was joined by more than 200,000 children.

But the real vitality was shown in the prizes, which were never better, never more ingenious.

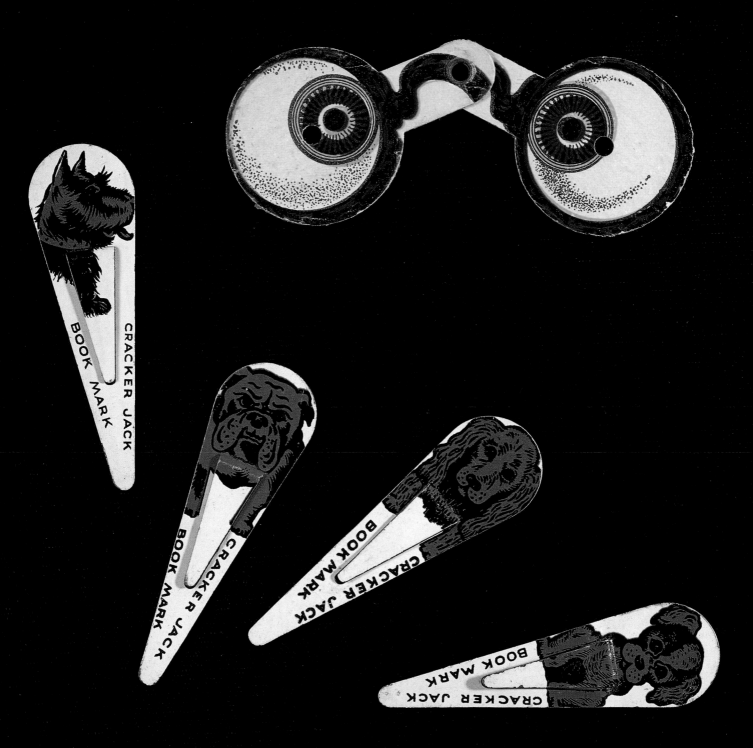

The above prize, in which Jack alternately writes and erases the words Cracker Jack, was the inspiration for this book's cover. Creating it out of genuine pictorial fragments, we wanted to make the book's impact the equal of the impact of a box of Cracker Jack.

This freight car was produced by the Tootsie Toy Company in two forms, one with black wheels, the other with white. One kind was sold in toy stores, the other found in boxes of Cracker Jack.

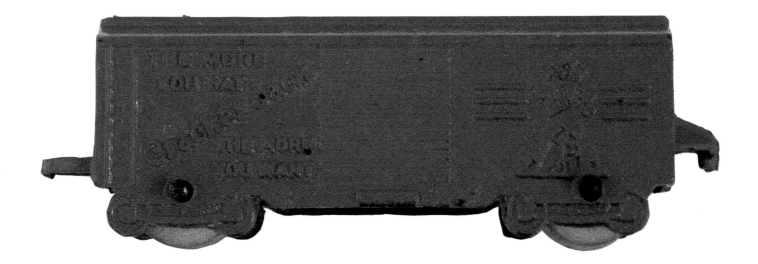

38

Instructions

1. Tie one end of each string to eyelets as shown in sketch "A"
2. Place eye-shade on forehead and tie the other ends of string together at back of head.
3. Be sure string is above the ears as shown in sketch "B" and eye shade will fit perfectly.

SKEEZIX

ORPHAN ANNIE

HAROLD TEEN

HERBY

CHESTER

MOON MULLINS

KAYO

UNCLE WALT

PERRY

SMITTY

Between 1933 and 1936 Cracker Jack carried forth its largest marketing campaign: "The Cracker Jack Mystery Club." During this period all the prizes were concealed in a separate cardboard section of the containers, and every box bore a question mark. The fortune wheel above was a prize from this era. The paper currency shown on page 42 and the thirty-one different coins were widely distributed. Children were invited to join the club, and almost a quarter of a million became members.

JIG-SAW PUZZLE
TEAR APART WHERE CUT. YOU WILL FIND
OTHER PUZZLES IN CRACKER JACK.
© 1931 The Cracker Jack Co., Chicago, Ill.

CRACKER JACK 512

A GOOD RULE — DEMAND
ANGELUS MARSMALLOWS
made by The Cracker Jack Co.

TWO TOPPERS
CRACKER JACK
ANGELUS MARSHMALLOWS

Cracker Jack

"The More You Eat —
The More You Want"

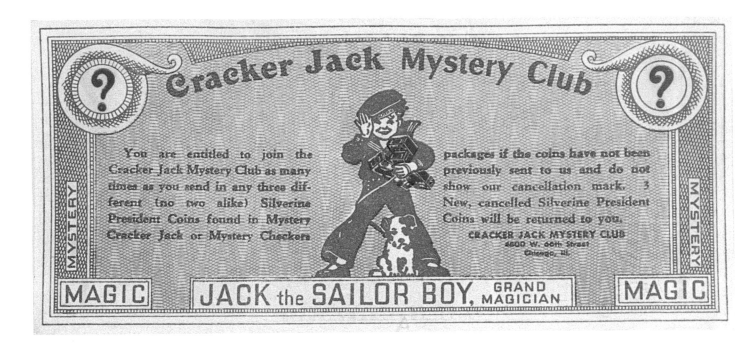

Cracker Jack Mystery Club

You are entitled to join the Cracker Jack Mystery Club as many times as you send in any three different (no two alike) Silverine President Coins found in Mystery Cracker Jack or Mystery Checkers packages if the coins have not been previously sent to us and do not show our cancellation mark. 3 New, cancelled Silverine President Coins will be returned to you.

CRACKER JACK MYSTERY CLUB
4800 W. 66th Street
Chicago, Ill.

MYSTERY   MAGIC   JACK the SAILOR BOY, GRAND MAGICIAN   MYSTERY   MAGIC

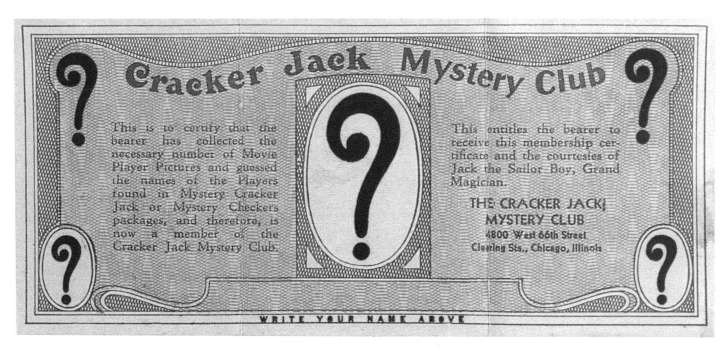

Cracker Jack Mystery Club

This is to certify that the bearer has collected the necessary number of Movie Player Pictures and guessed the names of the Players found in Mystery Cracker Jack or Mystery Checkers packages, and therefore, is now a member of the Cracker Jack Mystery Club.

This entitles the bearer to receive this membership certificate and the courtesies of Jack the Sailor Boy, Grand Magician.

THE CRACKER JACK
MYSTERY CLUB
4800 West 66th Street
Clearing Sta., Chicago, Illinois

WRITE YOUR NAME ABOVE

"The More You Eat
The More You Want"

Turn the Frog inside out-
place book or object on top
of Frog. When book is picked
up the Frog will jump.

THIS IS ONE OF A SERIES OF 6 BOOKS

BOOK 1

THE STORIES
of the
PRESIDENTS

George Washington, John
Adams, Thomas Jefferson,
James Madison, James Monroe

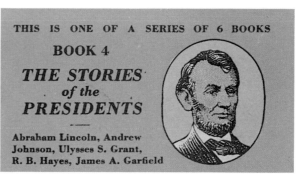

THIS IS ONE OF A SERIES OF 6 BOOKS

BOOK 4

THE STORIES
of the
PRESIDENTS

Abraham Lincoln, Andrew
Johnson, Ulysses S. Grant,
R. B. Hayes, James A. Garfield

43

SPEED DEMON
+ + +
STEP ON THE GAS – STIR UP THE DUST
YOU'LL BEAT THE OTHER CARS OR BUST!
BUT WHY DO YOU DRIVE AT SUCH A PACE –
WHEN YOU'RE REALLY NOT GOING ANYPLACE?

CRACKER JACK CHECKERS

SLEEPY HEAD
♡ ♡♡
RIP VAN WINKLE, MADE A RECORD FOR SLEEP
HE SLEPT TWENTY YEARS WITHOUT EVEN A PEEP
RIP NEVER KNEW YOU'D HAVE HIM TIED –
OR ELSE HE NEVER WOULD HAVE TRIED!

CRACKER JACK

MEANEST MAN
♡ ♡♡
YOU GIVE YOUR KID A PENNY TO KEEP
THEN STEAL IT RIGHT BACK WHEN HE'S ASLEEP
ON CHRISTMAS DAY NO PRESENTS APPEAR –
'FOR' YOU SAY, 'SANTA CLAUS DIED LAST YEAR'!

44

A minor campaign was the offer of membership in the "Cracker Jack Air Corps" and the opportunity to receive one's wings and four different balsa-wood airplanes. No one has yet identified any of these airplane prizes, probably because they were not marked "The Cracker Jack Air Corps."

46

The 1940s:
The War Years

World War II provided the flavor for this entire decade. As it began, Americans were living in fear and expectation that they would be dragged into the war raging in Europe. From 1941 through 1945 Americans fought in that war. So great was the drama, so high the stakes, so various the battlegrounds, that it seemed as if several decades were packed into this brief span. From 1946 on through the end of the decade, a type of energy was unleashed that follows only a life-and-death struggle. Everything had to be made new, everything seemed possible.

Metal flags, like the one that is shown here, were issued early in the war, when patriotism ran high and metal was not yet rationed. Later, all of the prizes were made of paper. The shortages of materials caused by the war effort set the Cracker Jack planners to thinking. They learned how to substitute ingenuity for the profligacy of The Golden Age. This cast of mind would continue after the war, and imaginative variations on inexpensive ideas have continued to this day to characterize Cracker Jack prizes. The introduction of plastic prizes, at the end of the decade, gives final shape to the future of Cracker Jack. Thus, during the 1940s, The Metal Age was followed by a transitional Age of Paper, which led directly to our time: The Plastic Age.

These violent scenes come from a set of cards that celebrate the heroism of winners of Britain's Victoria Cross.

The Bristol-Blenheim bomber on the opposite page was part of a set of cards intended to assist the amateur airplane spotter. Americans were encouraged to scan the sky and report any mysterious aircraft to the military. This Cracker Jack set included 24 airplanes that were from both the Allies and Axis.

The Bristol "Beaufort"

The Lockheed "Lightning"

ENGLAND   BRISTOL-BLENHEIM

50

The little plastic figure to the left, issued in the late 1940s, has a dual historical significance. One of the first injection-molded plastic prizes to be found in a Cracker Jack box, it was the cause of a minor furor. Rabid anticommunists, detecting a similarity in the figure to the appearance of Joseph Stalin, believed that Cracker Jack was being used to propagandize the youth of America. The company explained that this prize simply represented an old sea captain, but, nevertheless, it was withdrawn from circulation. This episode demonstrates how unfair anticommunism could be, for Cracker Jack has always been one of the most clearly patriotic manifestations of our national consciousness.

UNITED STATES of AMERICA

CRACKER JACK
TOOT TOOT
WHISTLE

Long may it wave!

BEND HERE TO STAND UP
OH, SAY CAN YOU SEE,
BY THE DAWN'S EARLY LIGHT,
WHAT SO PROUDLY WE HAILED
AT THE TWILIGHT'S LAST GLEAMING.

BE CAREFUL!

CRACKER JACK GOLF
CRACKER JACK

52

Plastic (a word used to characterize a group of man-made substances) has been around, in one form or another, since the late 19th century. In the 1940s, however, techniques were developed by which these synthetic mixtures could be injected into molds and rapidly hardened. Cracker Jack first used this process, and this substance, in the 1940s. It was ideal for a world of inexpensive prizes. Artists could cheaply realize their inventive intentions, and a great variety of forms could be made. From 1948 onward the company wrapped every prize individually.

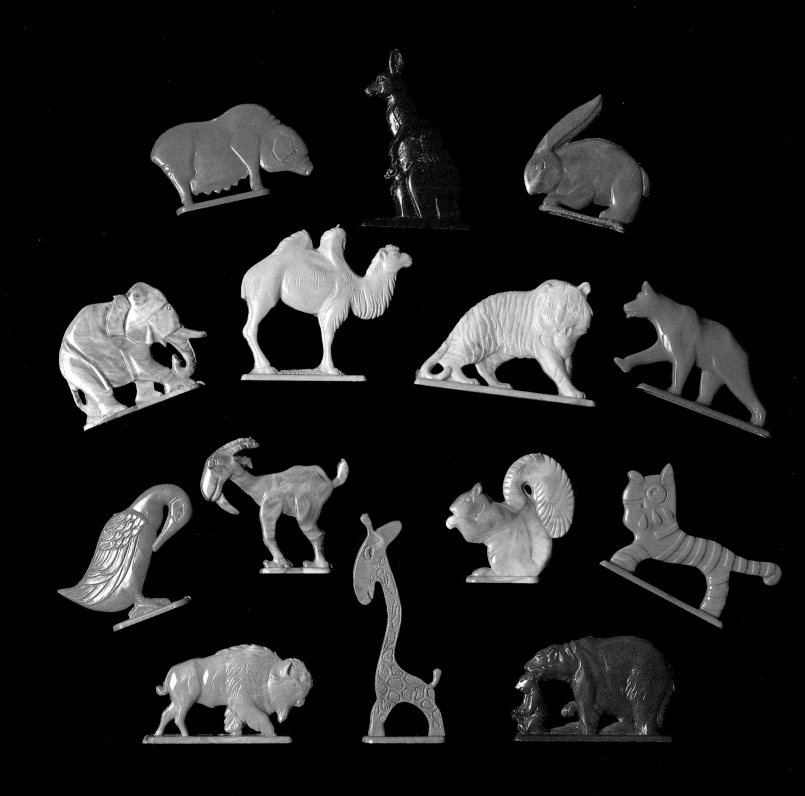

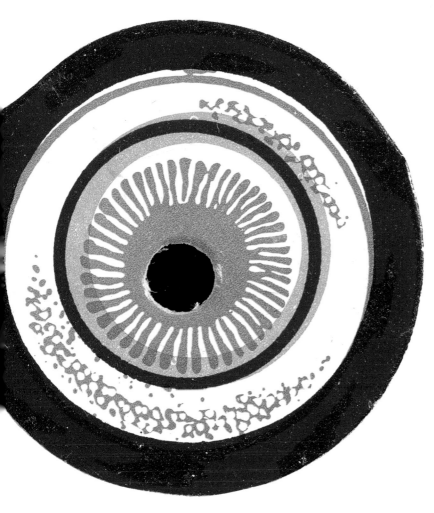

The 1950s: Plastic Profusion

55

The force of the Second World War was so great that its impact continued to be felt into the next decade. Americans, still recoiling from the face of destruction, tried to build a heaven on earth. Home building boomed. Consumer spending rose, and that helped create an era of prosperity. But many disturbing things also happened: Castro took over Cuba, the Army-McCarthy hearings were held, the Korean war was fought, and racial strife throbbed like a wound as the fight for desegregation went on. All of this encouraged the search for salvation through consumption.

Cracker Jack, as it always has, triumphed over the doubts of the time, and a joyful bounty of prizes was manifested. Cowboys and spacemen were enormously popular; the one interest rooted in our history and the staple fare of the ubiquitous TV, the other presaging the future. The low cost and easy manipulation of plastic led to a torrent of forms. As the whole culture grew and diversified, so did Cracker Jack.

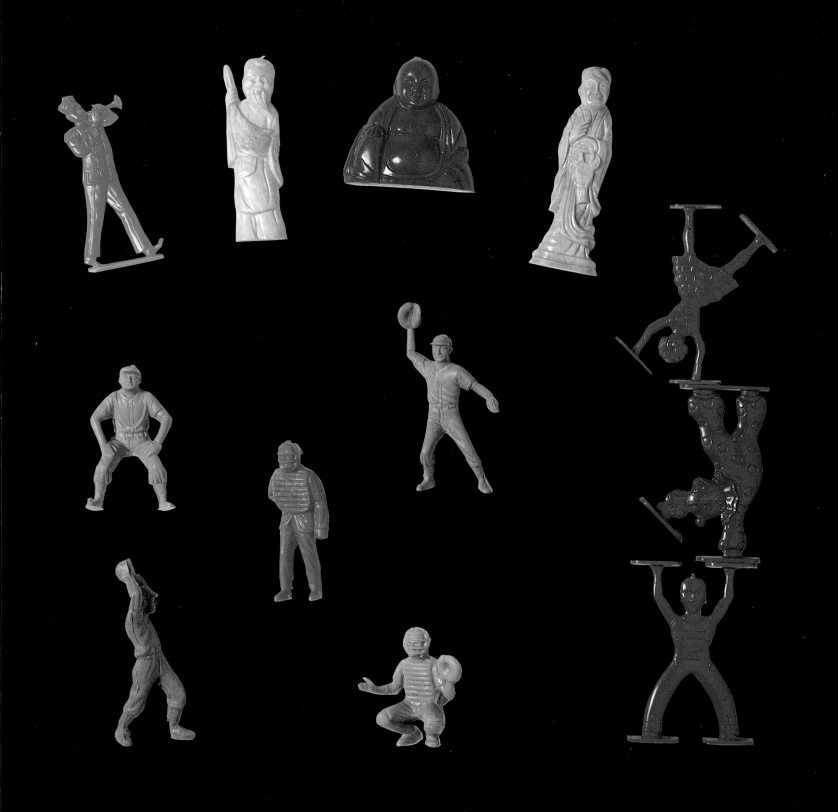

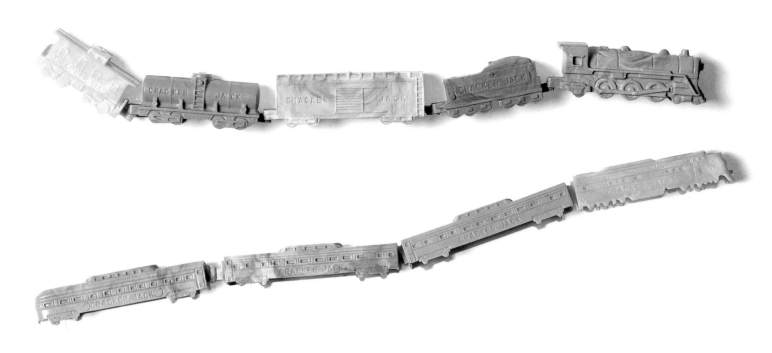

58

Santa Maria - 1492

Lightning - 1854

Cracker Jack planners and artisans imaginatively explored the possibilities of molded plastic. On these pages are shown but a few of the almost infinite variations they played on familiar themes.

One wonders why watch fobs were offered with these in the 1950s, when the pocket watch had become so rare an item. Furthermore, there is no evidence that Cracker Jack distributed plastic pocket watches, which would at least have given purpose to these curious items. All 26 letters of the alphabet were available.

61

TRICK MUSTACHE

Push out
both pieces

CRACKER JACK

Clip
to nose

MIDGET AUTO RACE

Spin the disk by
holding as shown
in the diagram.
The Midget Racer
that stops nearest
the arrow wins.

The Cracker Jack Co.

62

BIG SHOT

CANNONSVILLE, N.Y.

COW HEAD

KIOWA

IN MY TOWN
You're the
VACANT
BLOCK!

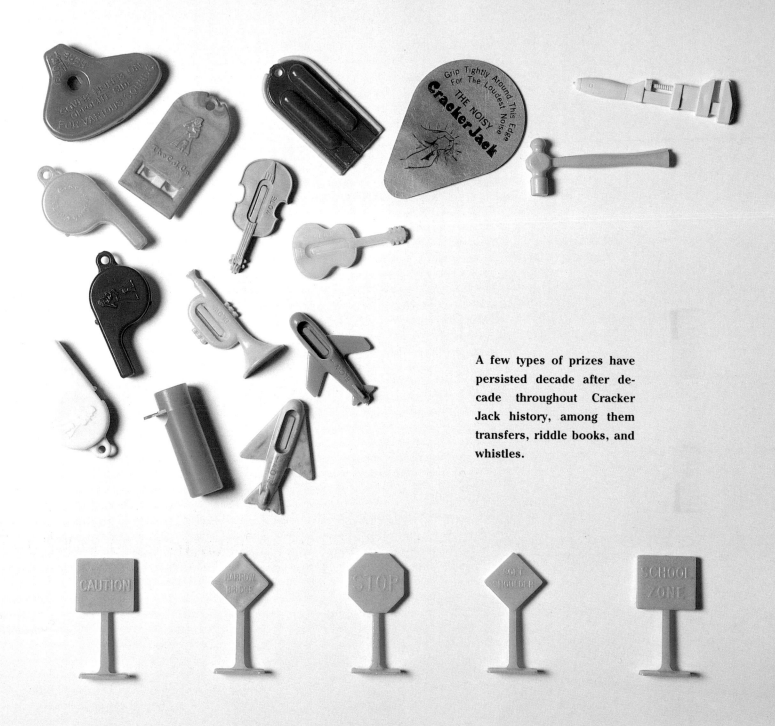

A few types of prizes have persisted decade after decade throughout Cracker Jack history, among them transfers, riddle books, and whistles.

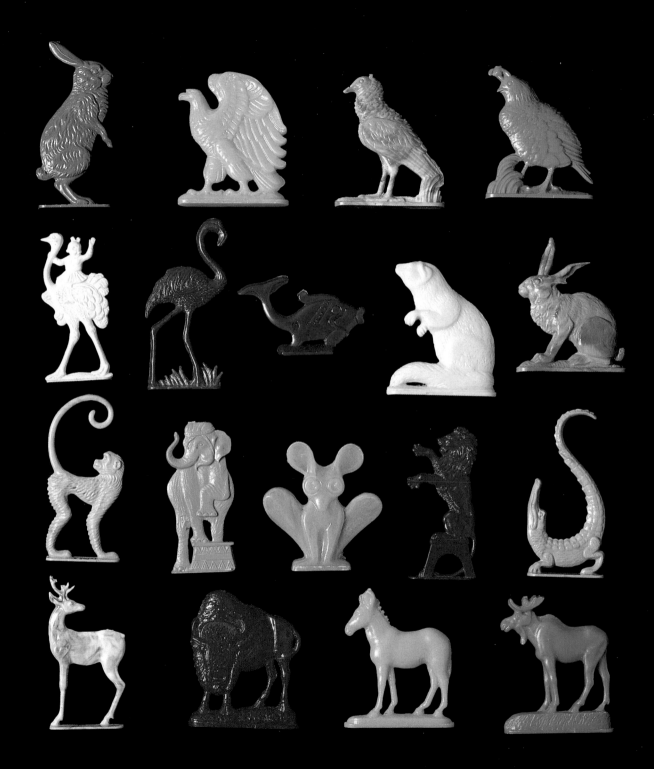

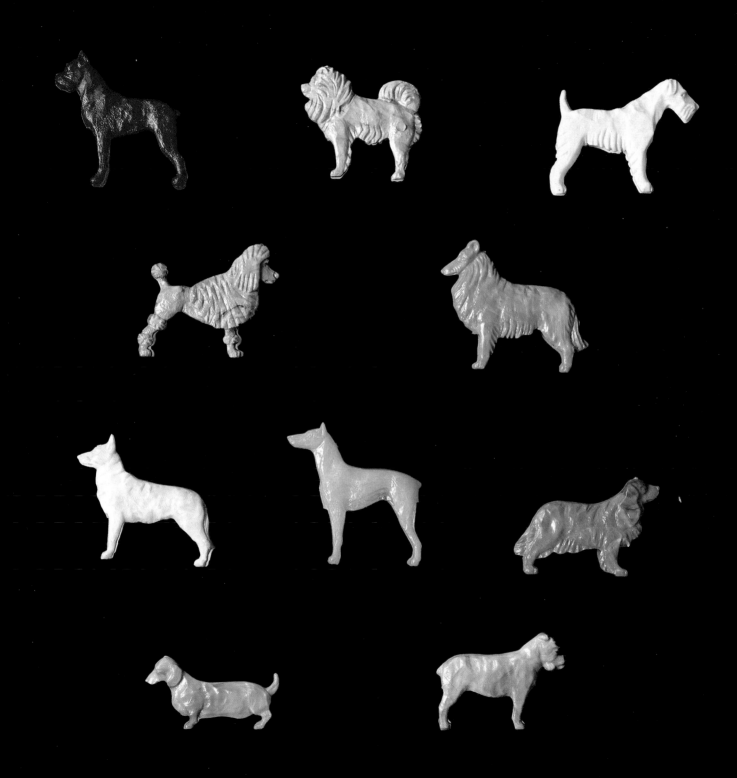

The 1960s:
Weathering the Storm

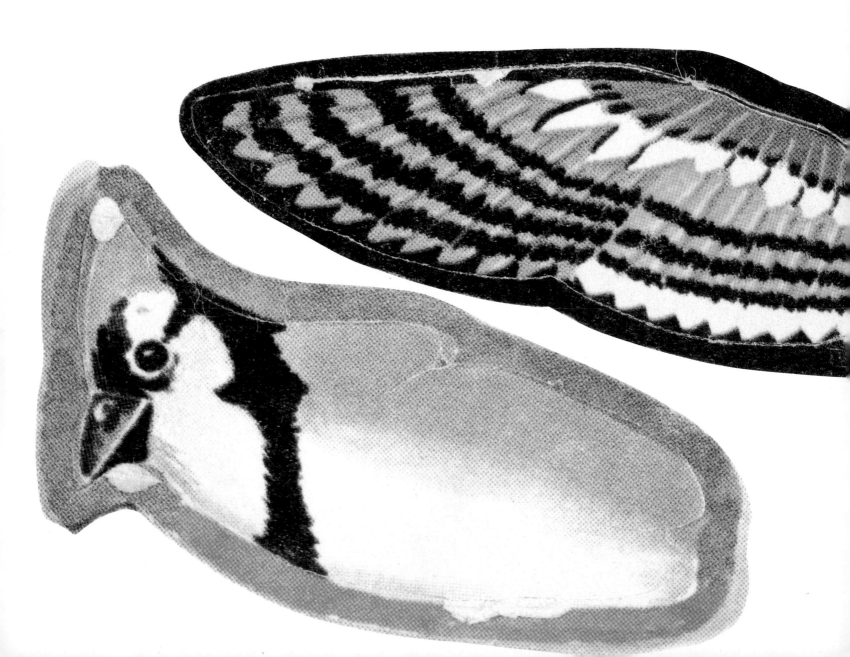

The '60s started on a hopeful note with the election of the young and vigorous Jack Kennedy. His assassination, in 1963, cast a tone of disillusionment over the entire decade; this was reinforced by the unpopular Vietnam War, which began in 1964 and dragged on and on. The nation was desperately in need of new kinds of heroes, and the various NASA triumphs in space gave them to us.

In 1964 Cracker Jack was purchased by Borden, Inc. The prizes continued to be various and ingenious. Plastic craftsmanship flourished, and because of it Cracker Jack was to create lovely artifacts, like the mummies pictured on page 73.

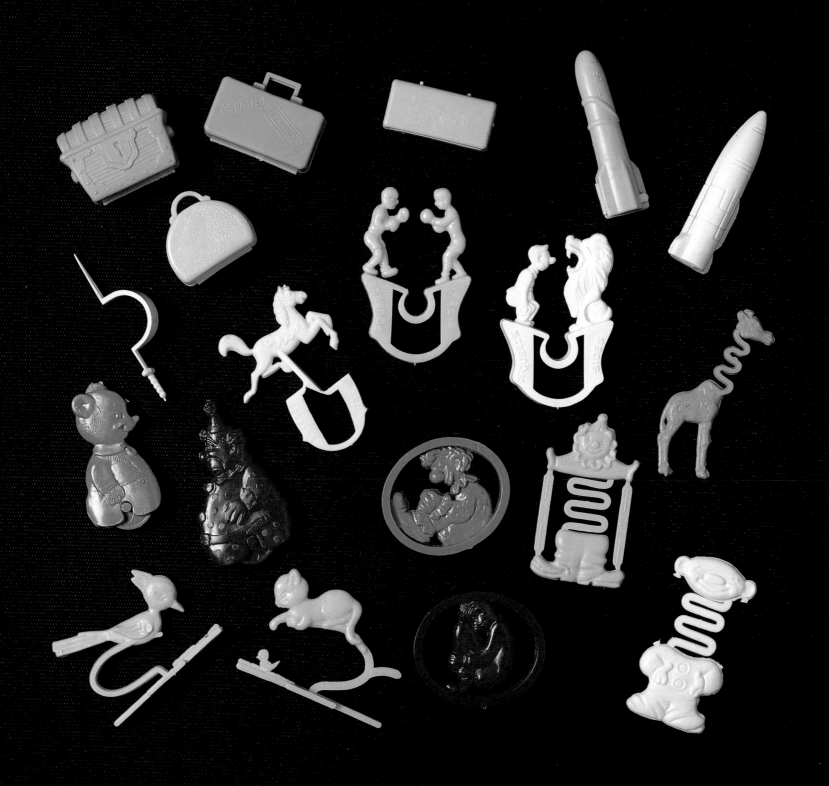

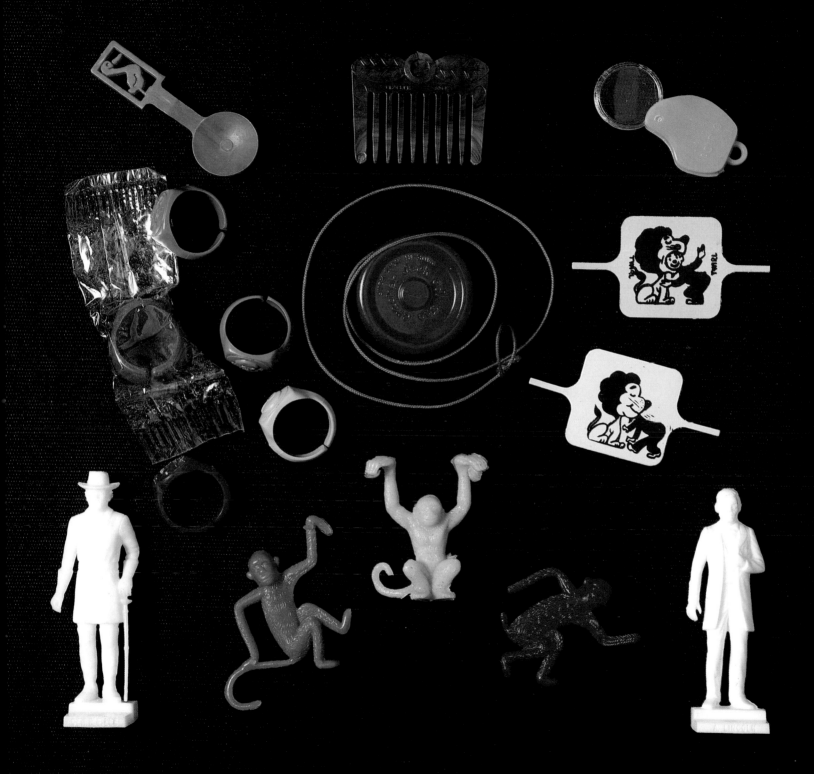

The transfers in the top row demonstrate, both by their content and design, much about the '60s.

At this time, with increasing frequency, prizes took on the general form of books. Here we have some characteristic examples: miniature comic books, paint and coloring books, notepads, flip movies, and the ever-popular book of riddles.

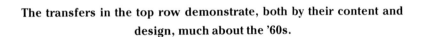

71

The Chinese boy, in the lower row, was the first Cracker Jack prize that I remember. My
collection was begun with a desire to find again the lost prize of my childhood.

ENCYCLOPEDIA OF
FAMOUS MEN
VOLUME NO. 4

ENCYCLOPEDIA OF
FAMOUS WOMEN
VOLUME NO. 5

ENCYCLOPEDIA OF
INSECTS
VOLUME NO. 9

ENCYCLOPEDIA OF
EDIBLE FISH
VOLUME NO. 6

ENCYCLOPEDIA OF
**GREAT
INVENTIONS**
VOLUME NO. 10

ENCYCLOPEDIA OF
**MUSICAL
INSTRUMENTS**
VOLUME NO. 11

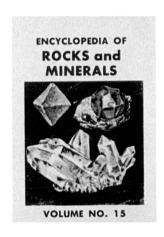

ENCYCLOPEDIA OF
**ROCKS and
MINERALS**
VOLUME NO. 15

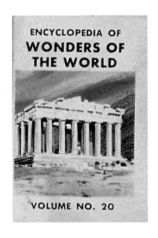

ENCYCLOPEDIA OF
**WONDERS OF
THE WORLD**
VOLUME NO. 20

Hello,
1980!

SUMMER BLIZZARDS

Hello, 1980!

**MAD SCIENTIST MAKES
HAIR CURL, DECURL**

Hello,
1980!

Hello, 1980!

72

When the Borden company took over Cracker Jack in 1964, its management wanted to try a few new ideas. One of them was complex plastic prizes that had to be assembled from parts. They proved unpopular and were abandoned after one year. Many people, expecting something immediately satisfying from their box, were baffled and frustrated by these prizes.

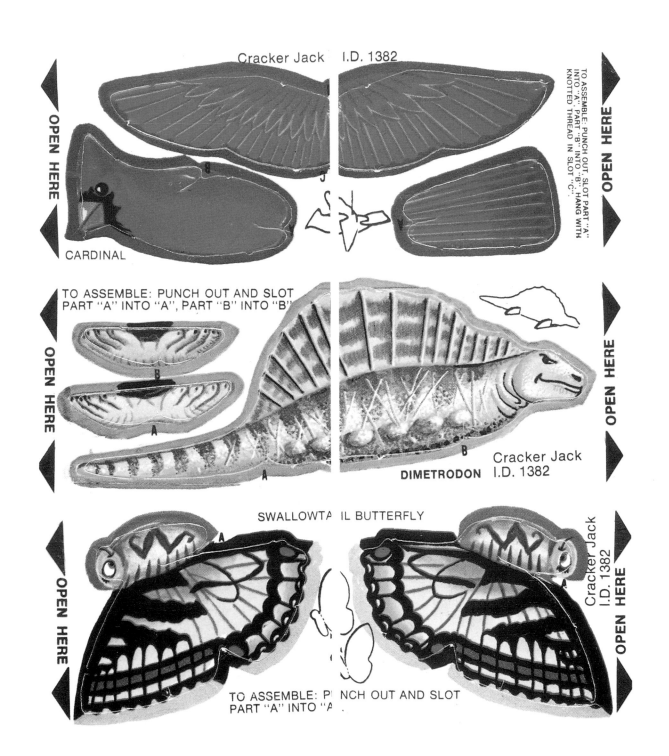

Cracker Jack I.D. 1382

OPEN HERE

OPEN HERE

TO ASSEMBLE: PUNCH OUT, SLOT PART "A"
INTO "A", PART "B" INTO "B", HANG WITH
KNOTTED THREAD IN SLOT "C".

CARDINAL

TO ASSEMBLE: PUNCH OUT AND SLOT
PART "A" INTO "A", PART "B" INTO "B"

OPEN HERE

OPEN HERE

DIMETRODON

Cracker Jack
I.D. 1382

SWALLOWTAIL BUTTERFLY

OPEN HERE

OPEN HERE

Cracker Jack
I.D. 1382

TO ASSEMBLE: PUNCH OUT AND SLOT
PART "A" INTO "A"

75

The 1970s: Within Strict Limits

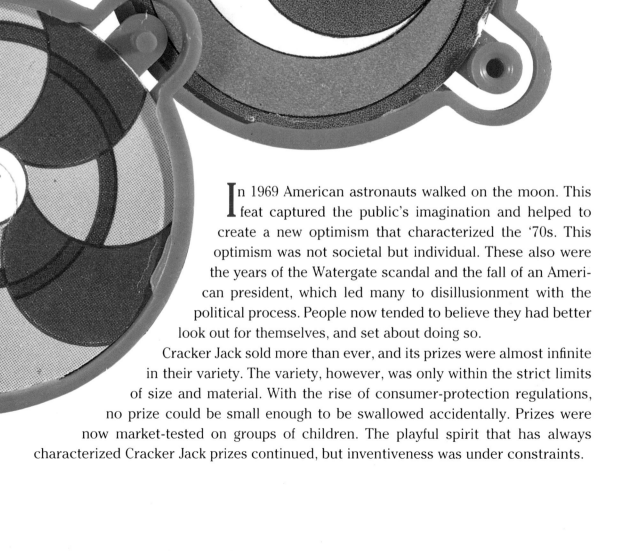

In 1969 American astronauts walked on the moon. This feat captured the public's imagination and helped to create a new optimism that characterized the '70s. This optimism was not societal but individual. These also were the years of the Watergate scandal and the fall of an American president, which led many to disillusionment with the political process. People now tended to believe they had better look out for themselves, and set about doing so.

Cracker Jack sold more than ever, and its prizes were almost infinite in their variety. The variety, however, was only within the strict limits of size and material. With the rise of consumer-protection regulations, no prize could be small enough to be swallowed accidentally. Prizes were now market-tested on groups of children. The playful spirit that has always characterized Cracker Jack prizes continued, but inventiveness was under constraints.

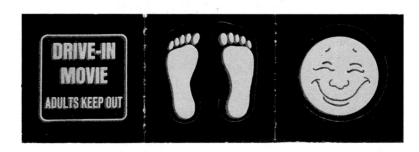

Psychedelic designs, like those in the top two rows, were frequent in the 1970s. The stickers, just below them, proved very successful; Cracker Jack issued around 40 different sets of these. The set below marks the first appearance of glow-in-the-dark prizes.

2. A group of cattle is a...

is called a...

2. A gaggle is a group of...

2. Which state is the smallest?

STATE SLIDE-CARD

ence became Presidents?

2. Who was the only unmarried President?

PRESIDENT SLIDE · CARD

answer

1. Band.

2. Herd.

Read question on front find answer on back.

CRACKER JACK DIVISION Borden Inc. Chicago, IL 60638 ID 1395

brood.

2. Geese.

answer

Read question on front find answer on back.

CRACKER JACK DIVISION Borden Inc. Chicago, IL 60638 ID 1395

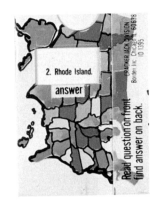

2. Rhode Island.

answer

Read question on front find answer on back.

CRACKER JACK DIVISION Borden Inc. Chicago, IL 60638 ID 1395

2. James Buchanan.

3. Martin Van Buren

answer

Read question on front find answer on back.

CRACKER JACK DIVISION Borden Inc. Chicago, IL 60638 ID 1395

3 tattoos

4 tattoos

TATTOOS

5

The slide cards are a new manifestation of Cracker Jack as teacher. The very popular tattoos permitted a child to frighten his parents into believing him disfigured. The captioned buttons, to the right, show us the attitudes and speech patterns of the times.

Tough Enough

NEATO

When in doubt...? DOUBT!

HEAVY

I'm Flip

RIGHT ON

DYNOMITE

GOOD STUFF

UP WITH UP

Down with Down

WHATS HAPPENING

HEY WHATS UP?

SUPER

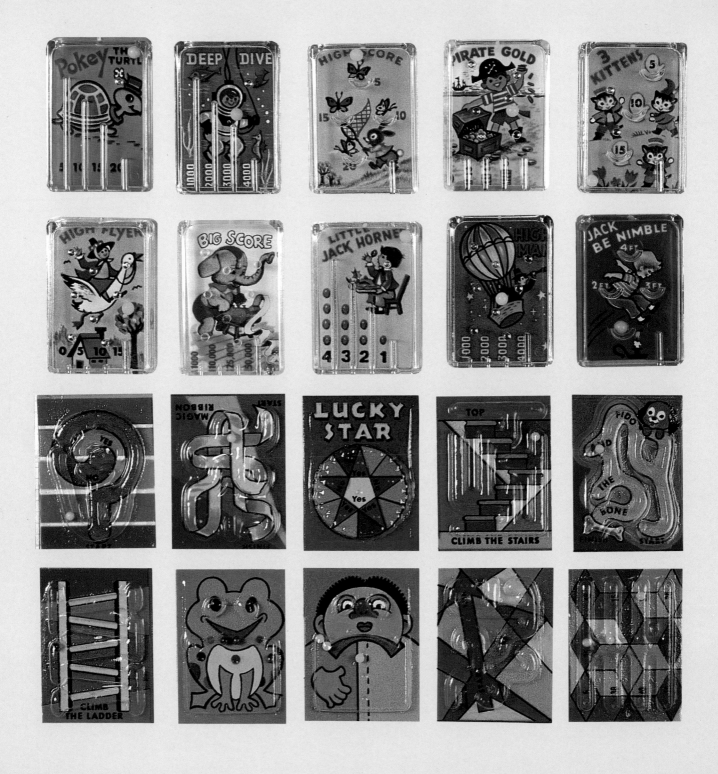

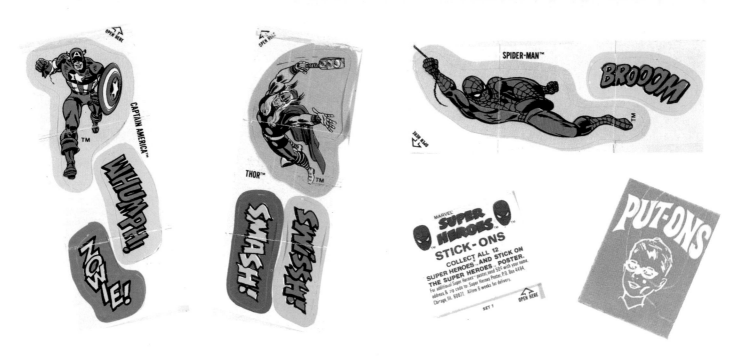

For the last three months of 1979 all boxes of Cracker Jack contained Marvel Super-Hero stickers as their prize. Despite an invitation to "collect all 12," there were more than 40 designs.

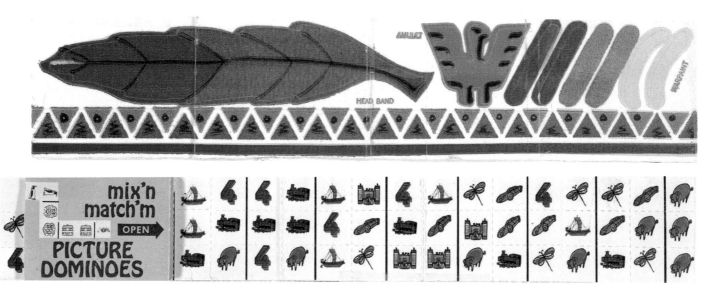

I served as Cracker Jack's official spokesman in 1981, and I met many people for whom a variety of Cracker Jack prizes had played significant roles at important points in their lives. When we were courting, my wife-to-be and I used to like to play Cracker Jack picture dominoes while waiting for dinner to be prepared in a restaurant.

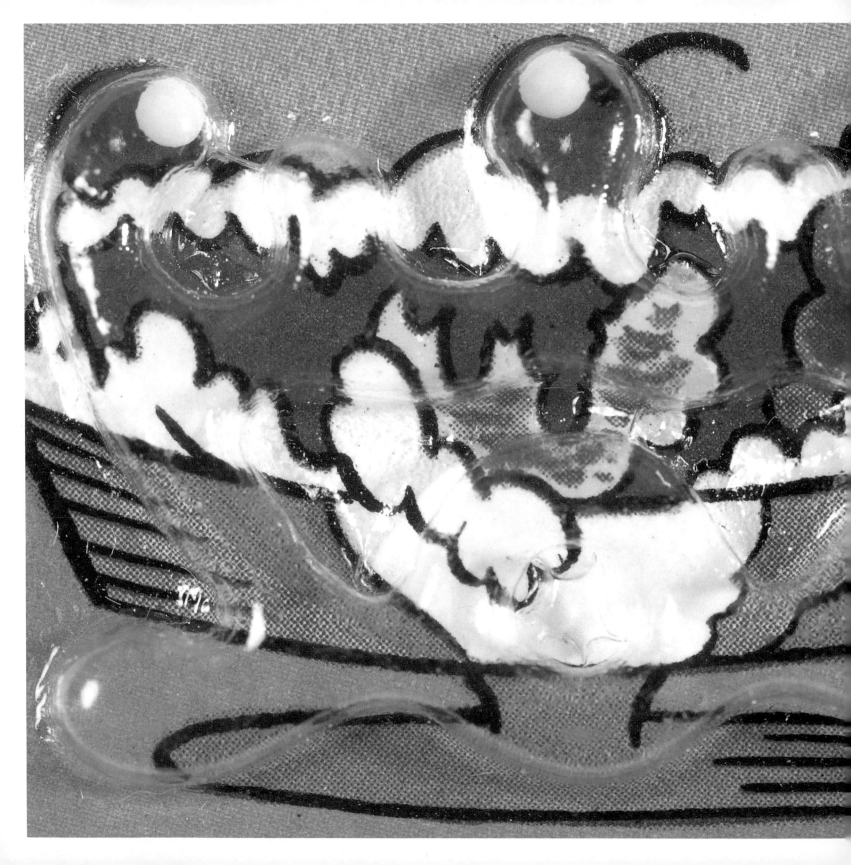

The 1980s: Instant Gratification and Disposability

As we look back over human history there seems to be an acceleration as the dates grow closer to our own. We can easily take a simplistic view of a decade's events when they happened in the 17th century, but in our own time everything is complex and contradictory. When history arrives at our own decade, our perspective is almost wholly gone.

As the current decade began, Cracker Jack intensified its promotional efforts, its prizes even outgrowing the box. In 1980 the company offered the lucky buyers of certain boxes $500,000 worth of prizes. One prize was a Mazda station wagon full of gifts. In 1981 Cracker Jack offered even more: $1,000,000 in gifts, including Winnebago motor homes. In 1982 and 1983 the company sponsored the Cracker Jack Old Timer's Baseball Classic, which was televised nationally. After this they settled down to being just good old Cracker Jack, with small thrills and miniature prizes. Who knows what the company's future holds?

Cracker Jack, as it always has, strides forward, absorbing the spirit of its times, and somehow transcending all obstacles. Grim aspects of our times such as the widespread preoccupation with horror movies and novels, or our growing concern over the spoiling of our world are given light-hearted manifestation in wall stickers and endangered species booklets. To those of us who prefer to search through a box of treats rather than the daily newspaper, Cracker Jack still offers delight, and, seen accumulatively, a kind of wisdom.

The creepy quality of some of these wall stickers, which were given out in 1984 and
1985, parallels the popularity of Topp's Garbage Pail Kids and the great success of
horror movies at that time.

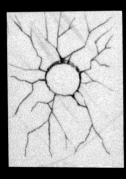

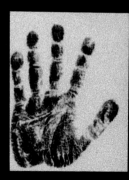

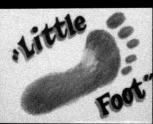

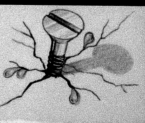

ZOO STICKERS of ENDANGERED SPECIES
(peel off backing)

GRIZZLY BEAR
HABITAT: Forests   NORTH AMERICA
ZOO DIET: Fish, apples, carrots, meat, dry dog food
WILD DIET: Plants, fruit, insects, small animals, carrion, fish
WEIGHT: 500 to 700 lbs.   **HEIGHT:** 7 to 8 ft.
FUN FACT: Both primates (apes, monkeys, people) and bears walk flat-footed or plantigrade (heel, toe, heel). Most other large mammals walk on their toes.

Despite its reputation as a carnivore, the Grizzly is an omnivore, eating vegetation along with meat.

(Special thanks to the Columbus Zoo.)

CRACKER JACK BORDEN, INC. COLUMBUS, OHIO
43215   B Series #42-4

89

Cracker Jack, in its own way, has always reflected the concerns of its times. Here there is mirrored our increasing concern that we are despoiling the natural order.

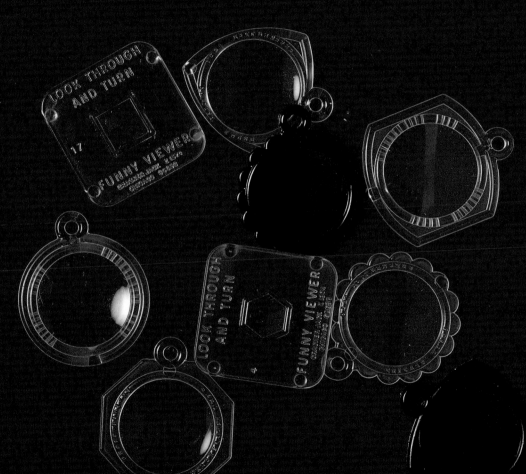

TAG ALONGS

Cracker Jack Series #48
Borden, Inc.
Columbus, OH 43215

1 of 15

PLACE OTHER SIDE UP

NEW TRANSFER FUN

Remove film. Place it CORRECT SIDE
UP on any paper surface. Use
DESIGNS to decorate letters,
notebooks, etc. by rubbing over them
completely with pen or pencil. Use
COLOR BAR for rainbow effects by
WRITING OR DRAWING over it sev-
eral times. DO NOT USE ON WALLS
OR FURNITURE.
CRACKER JACK
Borden, Inc.
Columbus, Ohio 43215

B-Series 59
#7 of 20

Collectible
Fun Fabric Stickers
Peel off and apply to
skin or clothes.

Cracker Jack®
Borden, Inc.
Columbus, Ohio
43215
B Series #57-3

These weather indicators really do what they say they do.

Weather Indicator

The fuzzy coating on the bird's sign......
changes color as the weather does. When it's
pinkish-beige, expect rain or high humidity.
When it turns blue, look for a clear sky & dry day.
Stand up near window or door—away from heat.

CRACKER JACK-B
Borden, Inc., Columbus, Ohio 43215
© Borden, Inc. 1979
Z-1406

Bend back to stand up.   SET 27

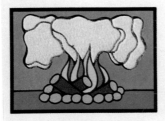

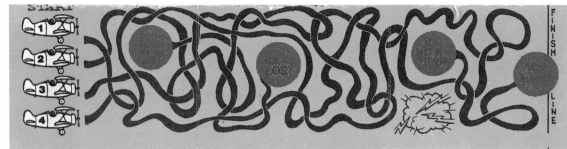

THE GREAT AIR-RACE GAME

ONE TO FOUR CAN PLAY.

START

1
2
3
4

FINISH LINE

SPEED LIMIT 55

Toy Surprise INSIDE

Cracker Jack®

CANDIED POPCORN AND PEANUTS

HERO

THE ONE MILLION DOLLAR QUESTION-

What to buy?

2,857,142 ice cream bars

ICE CREAM BARS   ICE CREAM BARS

25,000 kittens

500,000 pizzas

RIDDLE

(eye) (can)

read rebus

REBUS

CRACKER JACK DIVISION
Borden, Inc., Chicago, IL 60638
ID Z1396

COMPLETE-A-
SKY SCRAPER

DIRECTIONS: Remove stickers
from opposite side and
complete this scene.

CRACKER JACK DIVISION
Borden, Inc., Chicago, IL. 60638
ID Z1396

COMPLETE
-A-
MOTORCYCLE

DIRECTIONS: Remove stickers
from opposite side and
complete this scene.

GAS

CRACKER JACK DIVISION
Borden, Inc., Chicago, IL. 60638
ID Z1396

COMPLETE
-A- SPACE
SCENE

DIRECTIONS: Remove stickers
from opposite side and
complete this scene.

CRACKER JACK DIVISION
Borden, Inc., Chicago, IL. 60638
ID Z1396

X-RAY EYES

I'M SO TOUGH

I SCARE MYSELF

MAKE-A-
SANDWICH

DIRECTIONS: Remove stickers
from opposite side and
complete this sandwich.

CRACKER JACK DIVISION
Borden, Inc., Chicago, IL. 60638 ID Z1396

STAYING YOUNG

GETTING OLD

All of the notepads on this page were created by John Craig, an independent graphic designer, who, as an avid Cracker Jack collector, wanted to contribute something to the heritage of prizes.

1910s

1920s

1930s

1980s

These are representations of Jack and Bingo from each of the decades. You can see that both of them have changed. The earliest boy has a grotesquely large head, and his dog seems to resent posing, but they do have reality. The boy and the dog, like the box they adorn, have evolved, but still Jack greets us with a salute, and still we find in the tricolored box a compelling confection and a small surprise.

1960s

1940s

96

1970s

1950s